How To...

PLAY BLUES BASS

To access audio visit:
www.halleonard.com/mylibrary

Enter Code
7968-9115-4261-1072

ISBN 978-1-5400-1978-3

7777 W. BLUEMOUND RD. P.O. BOX 13819 MILWAUKEE, WI 53213

In Australia Contact:
Hal Leonard Australia Pty. Ltd.
4 Lentara Court
Cheltenham, Victoria, 3192 Australia
Email: ausadmin@halleonard.com.au

Copyright © 2002, 2018 by HAL LEONARD LLC
International Copyright Secured   All Rights Reserved

No part of this publication may be reproduced in any form or by any means without the prior written permission of the Publisher.

Visit Hal Leonard Online at
www.halleonard.com

TABLE OF CONTENTS

INTRODUCTION

Chances are that if you are reading this, you play bass and are interested in the blues. Maybe you're a beginner wanting to get started. Maybe you're a seasoned vet schooled in other genres who wants some quick authentic lines for a gig tonight or a shuffle next set. Maybe you know a few lines, but want to learn how to create new ones, or how to do more with the lines you already know. This is a place to start and a reference you can use.

Hi, my name is Mark Epstein. I've been privileged to play bass with Johnny Winter and many other heavy bluesmen over the years, which gives me an inside view of the blues world. Spending time making music with these artists has given me a real sense of history, how these artists feel about their music, what it means to them, and how it feels to play the authentic real deal.

Here's what I've learned.

It's all about *feel*. The blues ain't rocket science. If I were to write an instructional book on what *not* to play, it would be an encyclopedia. Ray Charles once said, "It's not how many notes you play, it's how much you put into each note."

Instead of progressive harmony and fancy licks, blues bass playing is about creating a great feel and locking it in. You're the heartbeat. You're the glue that holds it all together. You and the drummer are the foundation supporting the rest of the band, so simple and consistent playing are the key elements here. If you play a great line, repetition will only make it better. It becomes a "thing" unto its own. You tap into the spirit, and the musicians and artists playing with you tap into it as well—and love you for it. That's one way to get a lot of gigs!

Blues holds a special place in music history, as well as in American history and culture. American culture gave birth to the blues, jazz, and rock, and influenced many other styles. Some feel that our music is the best indigenous art we have to offer the world. Think of how much music in so many styles quotes the blues. Whether it's a vocal phrase, a guitar lick, or the I–IV–V progression as the basis of a song, the blues is everywhere when you have an ear out for it.

ABOUT THE AUTHOR

Few bassists come close to Mark Epstein when it comes to experience. He divides his time between recording and performing with many national and international artists, as well as producing, songwriting, teaching, leading creative workshops, and now, writing instructional books. His considerable experience, including positions as bassist for blues guitar legend Johnny Winter and Joe Bonamassa, gives him a unique perspective on playing blues bass.

Some other artists Mark has worked with include Dr. John, Edgar Winter, Robben Ford, David Crosby, Taj Mahal, Monte Montgomery, Maria Muldaur, and jazz heavies Dr. Lonnie Smith and Joe Beck. Other activities include performing and recording with Willie Nelson, working with Living Colour guitarist Vernon Reid on a movie soundtrack, producing a song for HBO's *Sex and the City*, and writing and producing a song featured in the Orion Pictures release *Speed Zone*. While living in Maui, Hawaii, Mark founded a weekly jam session visited by such luminaries as Prince, Larry Graham, and George Benson. He's even recorded and played some shows with tennis/media personality John McEnroe!

A new venture of Mark's is Buildsong™ (buildsong.com), innovating creativity and collaboration for business and education utilizing his music and production skills.

A solid groove player, Mark is quick to point out he plays *bass* on the bass.

How about you?

Links:
www.markepstein.com
www.buildsong.com
www.sxsessions.com

ACKNOWLEDGMENTS

Special thanks to my wife Diane, to my good friends and great musicians: Chris Hunt (guitar) and Paul Marchetti (drums) who helped me with the recording, and to all musicians out there keeping the spirit alive.

THE METHOD TO MY MADNESS

In this book and the accompanying audio, I'll show you some authentic blues bass lines and variations. I'll introduce a line by playing it through the 12-bar cycle and then take it through some different *idioms* (styles). You'll see how the same bass line works with different feels, and that only minor changes in the line can cause major changes in feel and groove. The trick here is not to memorize a lot of lines: it is to understand a few good ones and learn how to manipulate them to achieve the vibe you want. This is the power of the bass.

There are written lines (in standard notation and tab) and corresponding tracks for you to listen to. Each line is also described in "number form"—e.g., "1–3–5–6–7–6–5–3." Note that the numbers pertain only to the members of the *chord*. Since this is the blues, assume that all 7ths are *dominant* (i.e., a minor 7th above the root of the chord, like the F♯ in a G7 chord). In other words, if we were to play the line I've mentioned above with a G chord, the notes would be G–B–D–E–F♯–E–D–B.

Roman numerals refer to the chords themselves. In this book, you'll be dealing with the I, IV, and V chords in the key of G; namely, G, C, and D.

First, learn a line over the G chord (the I chord in G), then apply it over C and D (the IV and V chords). Then comes the fun part: apply the lines to the other styles, bearing in mind that you can combine different patterns to create longer, more interesting lines. You can think of these examples as good bass lines on their own, or building blocks for other creations. Happy hunting!

Note that all of the examples are in the key of G. If you'd like to play these lines in other keys, simply move the tab figures up or down the neck. For instance, if you'd like to play these lines in B♭, just move the tab up three frets on the neck.

There are longer audio versions, without bass, of the drum and guitar lines in different styles for you to practice with.

The shuffle and slow blues examples are played with a "swing feel" and the straight eighths and rhumba examples are played in "straight time."

Swing Feel (♪♪ = ♪ ♪)

Straight Time (♪♪ = ♪♪)

Note: The bass is mixed in a bit louder than normal so you can hear it all the better. Set your stereo "flat" for best results (i.e., the bass and treble at their middle positions).

Sometimes I take liberties with my notes on the audio—this is especially true during the *turnarounds* (at the end of the 12-bar progression, right before it's repeated) and at the end of the second time through. Go with the vibe that is right for you, be it what's on the page, what you hear on the tracks, or what you feel. If you're just starting out, you might want to stick to just the notes on the page.

Note: Track 1 contains reference notes for tuning: E–A–D–G.

THE 12-BAR BLUES

Throughout the course of this book, we will be working with the 12-bar blues. There are other forms as well (eight-bar and 16-bar). Since the 12-bar version is by far the most popular and recognizable, it's the most useful for study.

Here's the basic 12-bar blues progression.

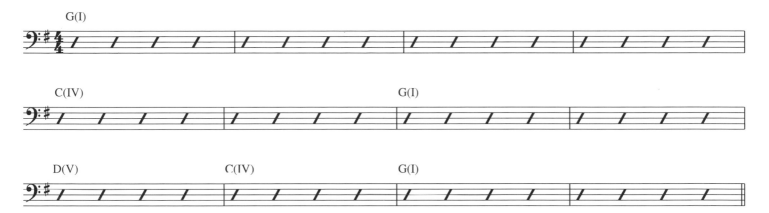

Notice that on the audio track, that last measure is always played with a I chord (G), but often (and you'll notice this on other tracks), when the 12-bar pattern is repeated, you'll hear a V chord (D).

Let's jump right in!

THE 1-3-5 THEME

The most obvious and popular blues bass lines are built from the notes of the triad (the 1st, 3rd, and 5th—1, 3, 5) of the chord being played at the time. A word for playing these notes separately (as opposed to all at once) is *arpeggio*. By playing the notes of the triad in different rhythms and orders, and adding notes here and there, we can come up with countless bass lines.

1–1–3–3–5–5–6–6

It's usable anytime. I often instinctively go to this line first. The last note of this pattern can be 6 or 5 (in other words, with the G chord, it could be E or D). Straighten out the shuffle feel for the straight eighths (blues rock) feel.

The entire 12-bar line is written out for you here, but for the other examples, it's up to you to take it around the cycle by mentally shifting the tab to play the line under the C (IV) and D (V) chords. To play the line under the C chord, move the pattern up one string, using the same frets as for the G line. To play it under the D chord, move the pattern up a string and up two frets. You can see this for yourself in the tab below.

Because these fingerings are pattern-oriented, you'll see that once you've learned the blues in one key, you've learned it in all keys. It only matters where you start from. Cool, huh?

TRACK 3
Slow Blues

TRACK 4
Straight Eighths

TRACK 5
Shuffle

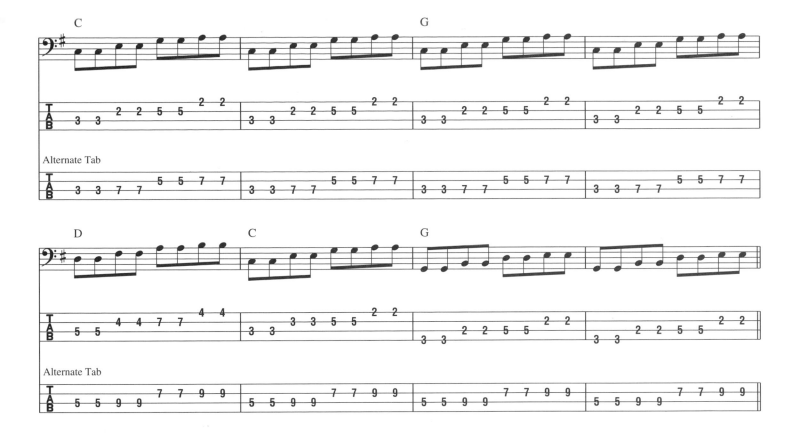

Feel

I want to talk about the concept of *feel* for a moment. I use the word a lot. Having a good feel is very important to becoming a good bassist or musician in general. It means that when you are playing, the music "feels" good. It's not enough to play the right note at the right time—you must understand the spirit of the music you are creating on a very basic level. It's almost a physical thing. It's not very easy to explain intellectually, but if you are aware of it, you'll know when things are feeling right. Trust me on this. You'll feel it.

Blues is a very "human" idiom. It's not about playing perfectly—it's about the music feeling good—getting the "groove." Things don't need to be exact or overly tight, but don't play sloppy on purpose.

When playing the blues, the feeling of the music is paramount; that's what all of the heavies look for. The "swing" of shuffles must really swing. That lowdown, slow blues number must feel lowdown. Like I've said, blues ain't rocket science. It's really quite simple technically, so the difference between a good blues performance and a bad blues performance usually lies in the feeling or lack of it.

One more thing: Don't sweat mistakes. If the groove is happening, anyone will excuse a wrong note. If the groove suffers because you're worried about making mistakes, the whole thing won't even get off the ground. Remember that the blues is from the heart, not the head. So go for it!

1–3–5–6–5

Listen to how this feel, which uses mostly quarter notes, is smoother. You may hear occasional grace notes in the shuffle and slow blues feels—hints of the shuffle feel within the quarter note feel. They give the groove a lift, but use them sparingly.

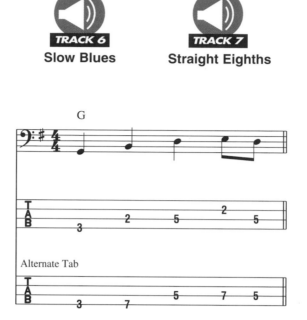

1–3–5–6–5

There's a small rhythmic change here to accommodate the rhumba beat. Try applying it to the straight eighths feel as well.

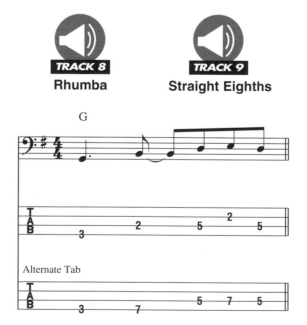

1–3–5

Here's a slightly simplified version of the previous example to accommodate the shuffle feel. Try it with other feels as well.

TRACK 10
Shuffle

1–♭3–3–5–6–5

Here we've got a ♭3 added into the mix. Blues is unique in that major and minor 3rds can appear in the same line. You've heard this sound a million times; this line gives the slow blues a '50s vibe. I think you'll hear a few songs when you try it with the other beats. Pay attention to the note durations on the audio tracks (especially in the slow blues version).

TRACK 11   TRACK 12   TRACK 13   TRACK 14
Shuffle   **Slow Blues**   **Rhumba**   **Straight Eighths**

Alternate Tab

1–3–5–6–5

Here's a great '50's 12/8 feel. It's also good with a straight eighths feel. Sometimes I play that last note as a 6 instead of a 5.

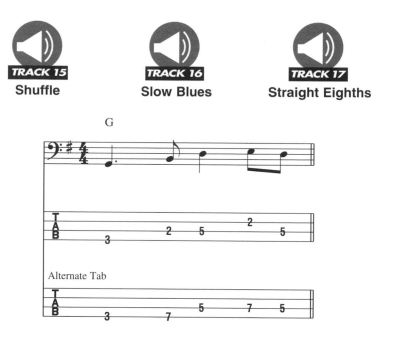

1–3–5 plus 1–♭3–3–5–6–5

Here's a two-bar pattern that combines two previous examples. The pattern can be played in either order (I play it both ways). *This is important:* As you can see (and hear), combining two similar patterns gives you a longer, more interesting bass line. The lines in this book are building blocks—it's up to you to try different combinations and come up with lines *you* like. Also, pay attention to how we handle the end of the blues progression, where only one chord per bar is called for. In this case, we follow the shape of the pattern instead of just playing its first half over and over again.

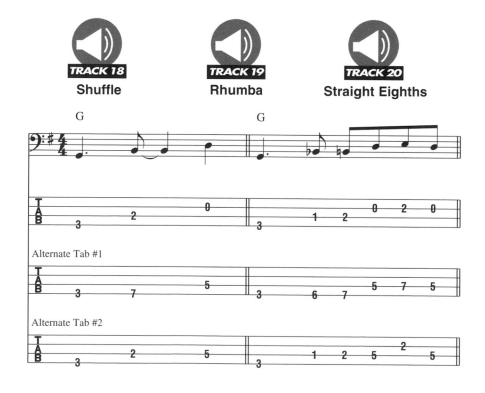

1–1–3–5 plus 1–♭3–3–5–6–5

This two-bar pattern is slightly different from the previous example in order to accommodate the slow blues tempo. As you can see, we're constantly tweaking our lines to fit snug with the drums. Again, these patterns can be played in either order.

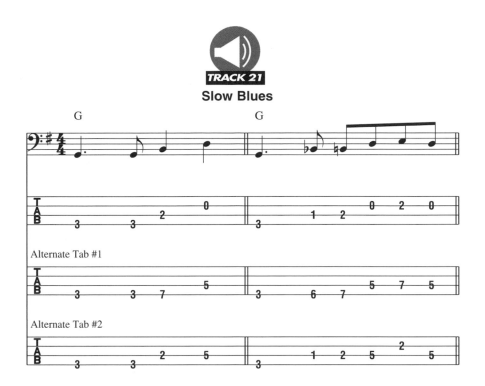

1–3–5–6–7–6–5–3

This is probably the most "obvious" swing line known to mankind. Some think it's corny, but it always works. As this is a two-bar phrase, notice that we're using only the first half of the line when only one bar of a chord is called for.

Special note: Listen to how you can "swing" a straight eighths groove (Track 25). By this I mean the bass swings while the drums don't. In the late '50s, this "in-between" approach happened when older swing era musicians teamed up with younger rock 'n' roll musicians. This is an example of bass and drums approaching the same music differently. It's a very cool feel.

13

1–1–3–3–5–5–6–6–8–8–6–6–5–5–3–3 (or 1–3–5–6–8–6–5–3)

This line can be played in both quarter and eighth note rhythms (it's written and played with eighth notes, as otherwise it's only one note different than the previous example). Try it with quarter notes as well. I included this line because to me it's an example of how changing one note changes the whole vibe. I find this line to be more "bluesy" as opposed to the previous example, which feels a bit more "jazzy." This is all subjective, but I find it is good to be aware of these impressions.

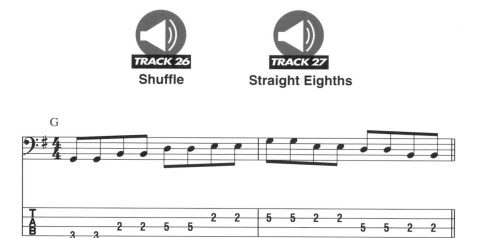

SHUFFLE AND WALKING BASS

The shuffle feel is played with swing eighths on the bass and walking bass is usually played with quarter notes.

Shuffle Feel

Walking Bass

The shuffle feel is bouncy. The bass plays what the hi-hat plays—every swinging eighth or 16th note in the measure. It sounds more staccato, more jumpy, light on its feet.

The walking bass/quarter note feel is smoother. The bass plays half as many notes as a swing eighths feel and with longer durations. It's more of a legato feel.

When "walking," you sometimes employ more harmonic options using passing tones and chord substitutions because of the jazzy feel you're creating. On the other hand, if you want a "down home," bouncin', traditional blues shuffle feel, stick with the triplet patterns and stay away from fancy passing tones and chord substitutions.

As the bassist, you have the ability to determine the impression and feeling of a song by how you approach your part—even if the other instruments play the same parts!

BOX PATTERNS

OK, let's get back to more bass lines. This next batch I call "box" patterns because of the shape your fingers make on the fretboard; some call this "Chicago style." All of the concepts discussed in the previous examples still hold true.

1–1–8–8–7–7–5–5

This is a great and popular authentic shuffle pattern that works for most anything else as well. You can't miss with this!

TRACK 28
Shuffle

TRACK 29
Slow Blues

TRACK 30
Straight Eighths

1–8–7–5

Here's a smoothed-out version of the previous line played with quarter notes. Add occasional grace notes to give the line a "lift"—but don't overdo it.

TRACK 31
Shuffle

TRACK 32
Slow Blues

1–8–7–5–5

This is a take-off on the previous line, with the rhythm tweaked to fit in with the rhumba beat.

Rhumba

8–8–5–5–7–7–♯7–♯7

Here's sort of an inverted (inside out?) version of 1–8–7–5. This line can gather a lot of momentum over time.

Shuffle

Straight Eighths

8–5–7–♯7

This is the same as the previous line but played in a walking bass style (quarter notes). Again, this line can gather a lot of momentum. I use this when I really want to drive a shuffle. Notice some grace notes on the track.

Shuffle

8–5–7

This is very similar to the above line, but the rhythm has been tweaked a little for the rhumba feel.

Rhumba

1–1–6–6–5–5–3–3

Here's another variation on a theme. By now you can see where we're going with all of this. This pattern works most anytime and is an often-used tool in my trick bag. You can also play the 1 up an octave anytime.

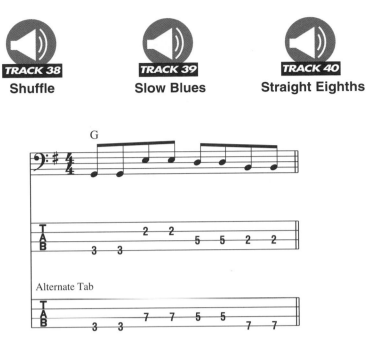

TRACK 38
Shuffle

TRACK 39
Slow Blues

TRACK 40
Straight Eighths

1–6–5–3

This is a quarter note version of the previous line, with occasional grace notes added on the track. It's very usable.

TRACK 41
Shuffle

TRACK 42
Slow Blues

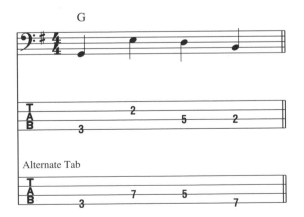

8–5–8–5–8–5–8–5

This line mimics the sound of the bass pedals of a Hammond organ, so it works great when an organ is featured.

TRACK 43
Shuffle

1–1–♭3–4–♭3

Here's a standard blues bass line that I'm sure you've heard in a number of songs.

TRACK 44
Shuffle

TONE

Tone is very, *very* important. You can play well, but that won't matter unless it *sounds* good—and it won't sound good unless you have a good tone.

Since it is your job to support and "ground" what is happening, your tone has to sonically do the job. Remember that in the early days of the blues (and sometimes now as well), the acoustic bass was the instrument used. A good upright tone is deep and rich. When the first Fender basses came along, they had flatwound strings on them to mimic the sound of uprights. Flatwounds are inherently deeper in tone than roundwounds. These days, most bassists use roundwounds, but they do have more of a "trebly" sound to them.

You want a strong, firm bottom to your sound. You are the anchor. You don't need too much high end or it can sound "clanky," but be careful about turning up the bass control on your amp too far, as too much bottom end is not a good thing either. Your sound can get so "woofy" that you'll lose definition—it can be hard to discern the pitches of your notes if this happens. You can also blow your speakers. You want enough low end, but not too much.

The rule of thumb I use is this: The louder you are playing, the less you need to boost your bass control. The higher volume will take care of the deepness you may be looking for. You want to fill the stage or room in which you're playing, but not overpower it. I always start "flat"—no boost or cut in EQ—and then dial to taste. Every room or stage is different, so don't be shy about experimenting.

Above and beyond all else, the most important element to getting a good sound is your technique—your tone is in your hands. Literally.

TURNAROUNDS

Turnarounds are chord changes and patterns that occur at the end of the 12-bar cycle. They are musical ways to get us to the V chord that signals the end of the cycle. There are many ways to get there.

Note that each of the turnaround examples below kicks in on the third measure on its corresponding audio track.

I–V

We can just play the dominant V chord instead of the I chord for the last measure of the cycle.

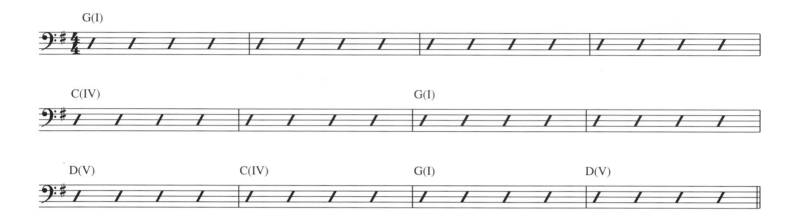

There are a lot of cool bass line variations. For instance, we can also play to this progression.

Slow Blues

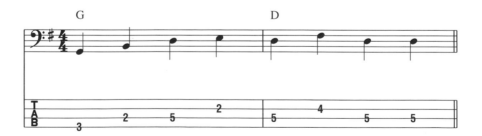

Here's another bass line for this turnaround. There are endless ways to do this—try out some ideas on your own.

TRACK 46
Slow Blues

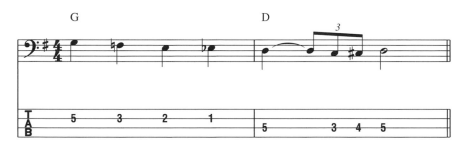

I–IV–I–V

TRACK 47
Slow Blues

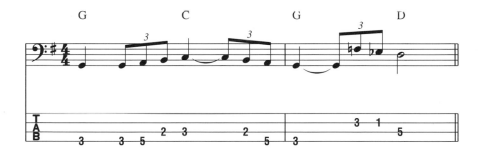

I–VI–II–V

TRACK 48
Slow Blues

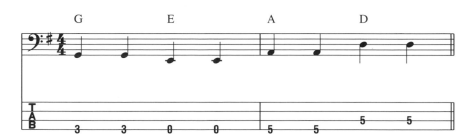

This one includes some cool *passing* tones (for more on passing tones, check out page 28). That A♭ leads right back to G.

TRACK 49
Slow Blues

If I–VI–II–V sounds familiar, you're on the right track: it's the progression for most of the '50s doo-wop songs. I find it interesting that the progression for one style of music can be a turnaround for another style. The more we explore the way music is put together, the more we can see this type of thing happening—so, learning one style of music can help us in others. After all, it's all music.

I–VI–IV–V

TRACK 50
Slow Blues

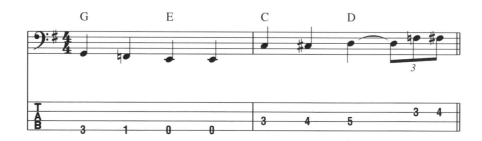

I–VI–II–♭II

Now, let's get a little fancy for a moment . . .

Slow Blues

I–♭III–II–♭II

Slow Blues

I–VI–♭VI–V

Slow Blues

As you can see and hear, there are many variations to this theme. Once you are used to hearing turnarounds, you'll start noticing them everywhere. Turnarounds give the blues an added dimension. They are important. The turnarounds you choose can make the music more jazzy, more sophisticated, more corny, or more "down home." How well a musician uses turnarounds tells me a lot about the person as a player.

As a bassist, you should be aware of what the other musicians are doing with their turnarounds. You may want to do what they are doing if it sounds good, or they may be looking to you for a little leadership in this department. Let your ears guide you. The more you do this, the easier it becomes. It's all about *listening*.

Check out and practice with these last four tracks. They are the four different grooves we have been examining, but without the bass. Try these lines and turnarounds. Make up combinations of patterns. In short, GO WILD!

Shuffle

Slow Blues

Rhumba

Straight Eighths

WORKING WITH DRUMMERS

Working with drummers—hmmm, now there's a can of worms. Where do I start? "It was the best of times, it was the worst of times . . ."

Working with drummers can be pure joy or a necessary evil, depending on the drummer. It's a musical marriage—bass and drums. You have to be on the same wavelength or there's gonna be trouble.

Rule #1: Play with the best drummers you can find.

For many reasons. First of all, a good drummer will have a good sense of time. This is essential for mental health as well as musicality, because if a drummer's "time" isn't good (slowing down or speeding up, etc.), it's going to be very frustrating. Playing with good musicians simplifies life a whole lot. When the music sounds and feels good, everyone's in a good mood and the music can do its thing. Also, playing with a good drummer will help you to grow as a bassist.

Rule #2: Having good time is not just the drummer's responsibility.

It's yours, too. If the drummer's time is fluctuating, are you just going to follow that bad time? *No— you both make up the rhythm section.* Keep eye contact, keep the lines of communication open. The rhythm section is a "band within a band." The rest of the group is relying on both of you.

Rule #3: Know the kick drum pattern.

You should base your rhythmic ideas on the kick pattern—that's where it all starts. Good arrangements are built from the bottom up. When you're building a house, you build the foundation before you put anything on top of it. In a traditional band, the same concept applies.

So, both you and the drummer have to rely on each other. With open ears and an open mind you can achieve that magical "lock" when the bass and drums play as one—one rhythm section.

PASSING TONES AND TRANSITIONS

Passing Tones

How do we get seamlessly from one chord to another? How do we make our lines sound more sophisticated or cool? Where do those other "professional" notes come from?

Well, without getting into the music theory involved, one answer is *passing tones*. These are notes not necessarily in the bass lines we're playing, but sound great on the way to the next chord.

By passing tones, I mean notes that are a half or whole step away from a note in the next chord. It just seems to feel good when a note in the next chord is close in pitch to the note played before it. That way, the change of chord is not so obvious. It sounds more gradual and smooth—in short, cool. As with grace notes used when walking, don't overdo it. Anytime you overuse a musical concept, it sounds amateurish.

The circled note below is a passing tone.

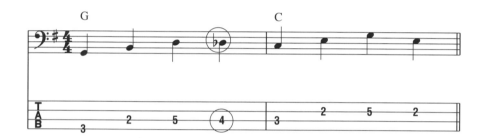

Try going back and using passing tones with any of the examples in this book.

Transitions

When working out a bass line and taking it through the cycle, we're sometimes faced with finger and neck position challenges. Always try to think ahead and set your hands up in advance of the moment you have to switch positions. This will result in smoother transitions, both physically and sonically. If there's an awkward move to make and you don't plan ahead for it, chances are that it will sound awkward. It's really worth working through lines with this in mind.

QUICK TECHNIQUE REFRESHER

As this book is not a "how to play the bass" book, I assume that you have some bass-playing skills, but I'd like to state a few concepts regarding technique. For those of you who know this stuff, bear with me. For those of you who are self-taught, you might want to check this out.

Left Hand: 4 Fingers=4 Frets

Wherever you place your left hand on the neck, you have four fingers at your disposal for fingering notes on the frets. The idea here is that with four fingers, you can play just about any pattern of notes in the space of four frets without having to move the left hand. You can "let your fingers do the walking"—the less physical movement you make, the better it sounds.

Put your left thumb on the back of the neck (about halfway up and at a 90-degree angle to the neck). Curl your fingers around the neck, placing each finger on an adjacent fret on the same string, with your fretting fingers directly opposite your thumb. This might feel awkward at first, but trust me; it will help you in the long run.

Right Hand: Alternate Fingering

It's a great habit and skill to use alternate fingering when playing bass. Most of us use our first and second (index and middle) fingers to play the bass. *Alternate fingering* means alternating between the two. By being adept at this, playing fast lines and maintaining endurance is much easier—and if it's physically easier to play, it will sound and feel better.

Practice in "Time"

As the bass is a rhythmic instrument, you should be in the habit of practicing in time. You should always be counting—tapping a foot, etc. I find that physical movement is always a good thing. I like using metronomes and drum machines to help me stay honest.

PUTTING IT ALL TOGETHER

How Bassists Fit into the Mix—Building a Bridge Between the Drums and the Rest of the World

Just because people can't identify what we do, it doesn't make it any less important. We're the glue that holds the whole thing together. If the drums are the motor of a band, we're the transmission. The car isn't going anywhere unless it's in gear, and we decide what gear we're in by our approach to our bass lines. We connect the drums to the rest of the world.

Ever listen to a band and one of the instruments cuts out or stops playing? Say, the guitarist breaks a string, a keyboard amp shorts out, or a drummer breaks a head. It sounds like something is missing, and it's identifiable. When a bassist stops playing, what happens? The bottom drops out. There's a big hole in the music, but most people don't know why. There's just drums and guitar and singing, but it doesn't sound like a band—it just sounds like a bunch of instruments.

If there is this great band, but the singer isn't cutting it, or the guitarist is out of tune, once again, it's identifiable. You can listen and say, "Great band, but tune that guitar up!" or, "Get some singing lessons!" But if the bass player's lame, people just think the whole band is lame. Why? Because the bass plays in the low register, and most people (some musicians included) aren't aware of what exactly is going on down there. Most people have to train their ears to identify low pitches accurately, and since most attention is naturally focused on the other instruments, not much attention is paid to the bass—until it misbehaves. At that point, people know only that something is wrong, but they don't know what it is.

We bassists have amazing power in a band. We can influence both the harmonic instruments and the drums, and no other instrument can do this as effectively. *This is our job*—we sit at the crossroads of rhythm and harmony. With this power comes responsibility: if we play irresponsibly, everyone suffers, but if we do our job properly, everyone looks good.

Music Is a Language

Music is a language—a language of sound. I don't believe it is sound for its own sake, but it is sound that is meant to be heard. It is expressive and can be interpreted. It has a vocabulary. We communicate emotions through music. Through the use of rhythm and harmony we can convey joy, sadness, anger, melancholy, and so forth.

I find it very useful to think in this way to help in deciding how to write and play music. Are my bass lines making sense? Am I getting my ideas across? Am I overplaying? The "overplaying" symptom is rampant—and remember that if someone talks too much, we just stop listening to them. Also, I know I respect people who speak concisely and with eloquence.

It's about ideas, not words. The idea comes first, and then we find the right words to speak or write down. Playing music is the same. If we don't know what we're trying to convey, all we're doing is throwing down notes. They may be good notes, but there won't be intent behind them. It's like speaking words that don't make cohesive sentences. To make a bass line really work, you must know what you're trying to say—only then will you know if you're playing the right notes, in the right rhythm, and with the right phrasing. That's when it really comes together. Without intent and understanding of what you're trying to accomplish, it's hit or miss at best.

Listening

I also want to speak about something that seems so obvious and needless to bring up: LISTENING. We're in the business of sound, so obviously one would think that listening should be a big part of what we do. Without good listening skills, we wouldn't hear and understand what the other musicians are playing. And how would we know what to play ourselves?

It sounds silly, but I can't tell you how many musicians on all levels don't listen enough. They're too wrapped up in themselves and what they're playing. But what if their playing is inappropriate—too loud, too busy, or even in the wrong key? Believe me, this happens. It's crazy but true—musicians not using their ears! Can you imagine an artist painting with his or her eyes closed?

So keep this in mind when making musical decisions:

Music is a language. Learn how to listen as well as how to speak.

BASS BUILDERS

A series of technique book/CD packages created for the purposeful building and development of your chops. Each volume is written by an expert in that particular technique. And with the inclusion of audio, the added dimension of hearing exactly how to play particular grooves and techniques make these truly like private lessons.

BASS AEROBICS
by Jon Liebman
00696437 Book/Online Audio $19.99

BASS FITNESS –
AN EXERCISING HANDBOOK
by Josquin des Prés
00660177.. $10.99

BASS FOR BEGINNERS
by Glenn Letsch
00695099 Book/CD Pack....................................... $19.95

BASS GROOVES
by Jon Liebman
00696028 Book/Online Audio $19.99

BASS IMPROVISATION
by Ed Friedland
00695164 Book/Online Audio $17.95

BLUES BASS
by Jon Liebman
00695235 Book/CD Pack....................................... $19.95

BUILDING ROCK BASS LINES
by Ed Friedland
00695692 Book/CD Pack....................................... $17.95

BUILDING WALKING BASS LINES
by Ed Friedland
00695008 Book/Online Audio $19.99

RON CARTER –
BUILDING JAZZ BASS LINES
00841240 Book/CD Pack....................................... $19.95

DICTIONARY OF BASS GROOVES
by Sean Malone
00695266 Book/Online Audio $14.95

EXPANDING WALKING BASS LINES
by Ed Friedland
00695026 Book/CD Pack....................................... $19.95

FINGERBOARD HARMONY
FOR BASS
by Gary Willis
00695043 Book/Online Audio $17.95

FUNK BASS
by Jon Liebman
00699348 Book/CD Pack....................................... $19.99

FUNK/FUSION BASS
by Jon Liebman
00696553 Book/CD Pack....................................... $19.95

HIP-HOP BASS
by Josquin des Prés
00695589 Book/CD Pack....................................... $15.99

JAZZ BASS
by Ed Friedland
00695084 Book/Online Audio $17.99

JERRY JEMMOTT –
BLUES AND RHYTHM &
BLUES BASS TECHNIQUE
00695176 Book/CD Pack....................................... $17.95

JUMP 'N' BLUES BASS
by Keith Rosier
00695292 Book/CD Pack....................................... $16.95

THE LOST ART OF
COUNTRY BASS
by Keith Rosier
00695107 Book/CD Pack....................................... $19.95

PENTATONIC SCALES
FOR BASS
by Ed Friedland
00696224 Book/Online Audio $19.99

REGGAE BASS
by Ed Friedland
00695163 Book/Online Audio $16.95

'70S FUNK & DISCO BASS
by Josquin des Prés
00695614 Book/Online Audio $16.99

SIMPLIFIED SIGHT-READING
FOR BASS
by Josquin des Prés
00695085 Book/Online Audio $17.99

6-STRING BASSICS
by David Gross
00695221 Book/CD Pack....................................... $12.95

HAL•LEONARD®

www.halleonard.com

Prices, contents and availability subject to change without notice; All prices are listed in U.S. funds

1216